A WOLRD OF LIGHT, THE COTE D'AZUR AND THE HILL-COUNTRY

Also available in English

- THE RIVIERA OF CHARLES NEGRE,
  FIRST PHOTOGRAPHS OF THE COTE D'AZUR
  Text by Joseph Nègre

- RECIPES FROM PROVENCE
  Andrée Maureau

- LOOKING AND COOKING IN PROVENCE
  Gerald Clayton

- THE PERCHED VILLAGES OF THE ALPES-MARITIMES (vol 2,3,4)
  S. & E. Guinsberg

- THE CANAL OF THE MIDI AND PIERRE-PAUL RIQUET
  Jacques Morand

- COSTUMES OF MOROCCO
  Jean Besancenot

ISBN 2-85744-891-0
© Édisud, La Calade, 13090 Aix-en-Provence, France, 1996.
Tous droits réservés.

A WORLD OF LIGHT
The Côte d'Azur
and the hill-country

Photographs
Jacques Schlienger

Translation Jill Harry

Édisud
La Calade, 13090 Aix-en-Provence, France

With thanks to

to Mr. Chaudoreille, for his confidence

to Mrs. Sylvie Girardet, for writing the texts

and Barbara, my wife, for her collaboration

FOREWORD

Photography is not what I do for a living, but something I've always loved. On my wanderings I share my discoveries with my family and hope that my daughters will keep fond and happy memories of these long days spent together, so that later on they'll tell the tale…

« When we were children, we often set off on weekends to discover landscapes that Daddy enthusiastically fed into his cameras. His deep-rooted need for light and images involved a marathon which started very early in the morning. How many times were my sister and I lifted out of bed and installed in the car when it was still completely dark ?

We learnt early on that the first rays of sunlight have a magical effect on the countryside, revealing its colours and reliefs. We drove for miles along steep and winding roads to reach tiny hill-top villages. We scudded our shoes along hundreds of narrow streets, splashing our hands in all the cool-water fountains we could find. But what we liked best was searching for a bakery where Daddy bought brioches flavoured with orange-blossom and small loaves stuffed with olives.

Each little alleyway, the tiniest dead end, were always paid a visit. We learnt how to observe everything, the doors, stones and trees…, a tiny detail would suddenly take on great importance beneath the fiery glow of the sun. We played on the beaches, had picnics on the mountain tops. We were bitterly cold when the winter Mistral began to blow, hot when the rocks absorbed the burning summer sun. We were also really frightened by the lightning of an unexpected storm that made us to race back to the car.

But during all these experiences, we watched the magnificent chopping and changing of the sky and clouds, the play of light and shade on the hills. We smelled the fragrance of wet earth, wild thyme and jasmine. We listened to the pebbles being sucked back beneath the waves, the song of the cicadas, the silence of the mountain peaks.

Our father's photos were nourished by these enchanted moments and from all those years of wandering we have kept thousands of images, thousands of impressions and vibrations, which made us fall so eternally in love with the land in which we live ! »

J. SCHLIENGER

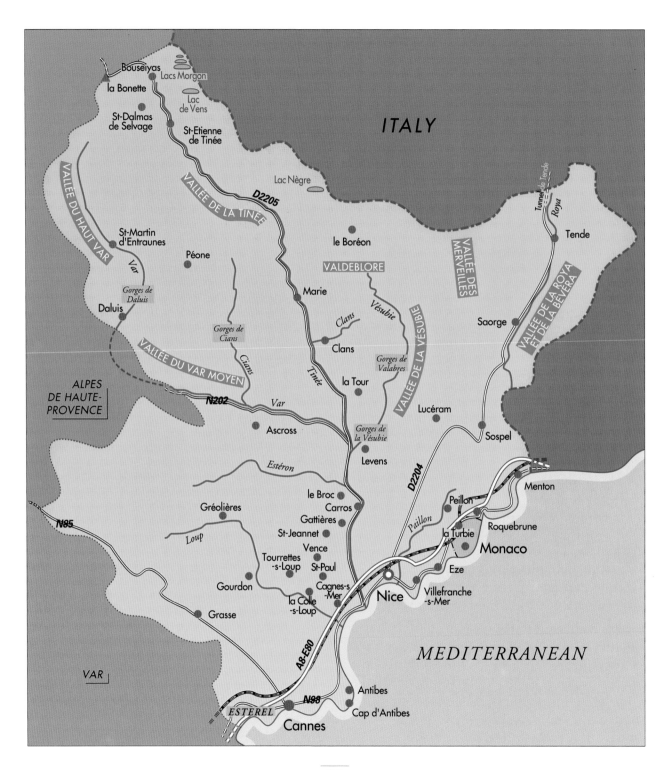

ITALY

MEDITERRANEAN

Bouseiyas
Lacs Morgon
la Bonette
Lac de Vens
St-Dalmas de Selvage
St-Etienne de Tinée

VALLÉE DU HAUT VAR
VALLÉE DE LA TINÉE
D2205

Lac Nègre

Tunnel de Tende
Roya
Tende

St-Martin d'Entraunes
Péone

le Boréon
VALDEBLORE

VALLÉE DES MERVEILLES

VALLÉE DE LA ROYA ET DE LA BÉVÉRA

Var

Gorges de Daluis
Daluis

Marie

Vésubie

Saorge

Gorges de Cians

Clans
Clans
Tinée

VALLÉE DE LA VÉSUBIE

VALLÉE DU VAR MOYEN

Cians

la Tour

Gorges de Valabres

ALPES DE HAUTE-PROVENCE

N202
Var

Gorges de la Vésubie

Lucéram

Sospel

Ascross

Levens

Estéron

D2204

Menton

le Broc
Carros
Gattières

Peillon

Roquebrune

Gréolières

Paillon

la Turbie
Monaco

N85

Loup

St-Jeannet

Vence

Eze

Gourdon

Tourrettes-s-Loup
St-Paul

Cagnes-s-Mer

Villefranche-s-Mer

la Colle-s-Loup

Nice

Grasse

VAR

A8-E80

ESTEREL
N98
Antibes

Cap d'Antibes

Cannes

INTRODUCTION

Alpæ Maritimæ, that's the very sensible name given to the region by the Romans in their day... The Maritime Alps, a *département* or county appropriately named, since its great originality comes precisely from the fact that here the coast and mountains combine to form one single region... and what a region, at that !

An azure blue sea, an immense bay bordering green hillsides dotted with ochre rooftops and colourful façades..., all mounted like a sparkling jewel in the midst of a semi-circle of mountains whose proud and jagged peaks are often capped with snow. So many contrasts, so many contradictions even, exist side by side to compose this magnificent tableau, a veritable stage-set open to the sky, as witnessed by Jacques Schlienger's photographs.

And yet history, several centuries ago, had decided differently ; in 1388, this fine geographic entity was split in two when what was then the County of Nice was separated from Provence and attached to the County of Savoy. It was only five centuries later, in 1860, that the *département* was pieced back together, thanks to the reunification of the County of Nice – which became part of France – with the *arrondissement* of Grasse. Later on, in 1947, the Alpes-Maritimes recuperated Tende and La Brigue, together with the Mercantour nature reserve, thus recovering its original

boundaries and the name Antiquity had given it. Beyond this re-found geographic unity, the Alpes-Maritimes can also be defined as a succession of "localities" which have all, in their own way, preserved their customs, dialects and ancient traditions. Whether they are *niçois, grassois* or *vençois*, all these localities are deeply attached to their own identities, have a story to tell and a richly varied palette of scenery.

The coastal region to the south boasts a hinterland fragrant with lavender and jasmine. To the west, the Pré-Alpes of Grasse are composed of plateaux, low-altitude mountain chains, and those very deep gorges cut by the Loup and Estéron rivers. To the east, the Pré-Alpes behind Nice surround the watersheds of the Paillon. Last but not least, the high mountains and their deep valleys (of the Var, Tinée, Bévéra, Roya, Vésubie), all quite different, extend their invitation to make edifying and spectacular discoveries, thanks in particular to the National Mercantour Park, a nature reserve purposely created to preserve the site's extraordinary heritage... and its marvels !

This book proposes a visual stroll within the region's 4,294 square kilometres, a "photographic escapade" through time and space. This is a land characterized by light and colour where reliefs clash with each other, where the ground rises very rapidly from sea-level to peaks of 3,000 metres, and the rugged universe of the high mountain region skirts the more rounded lines of the plain and coast. As far as passing time is concerned, it is visible everywhere in these diverse landscapes, in the depths of gorges, at the highest point of hill-top villages, and in fortified walls such as those you'll see at the heart of ancient towns with their mazes of narrow streets.

THE "HAUT PAYS"

Our photo-album begins with the grandiose scenery of the high mountain region. Jacques Schlienger's photos in fact give priority to this part of the Alpes-Maritimes, too little known and often wrongly considered as a mere backcloth for a more prestigious shoreline.

And yet, beyond the mountain passes and sign-posted pathways, this region, so hostile at first sight, contains hidden treasures. From peak to peak, from lake to lake, from one valley to the next, you'll discover fantastic itineraries revealing all the diversity of this high mountain area.

The Haut Pays is also an open book about rural life and how it has survived for thousands of years. From snow-capped massifs to flower-filled Alpine pastures, one comes upon abrupt slopes whose terraced embankments are carefully tended, inch by inch, to reclaim usable land from the rugged mountains.

Sheep-rearing, the oldest of man's activities, has been the most successful survivor in this austere and restrictive environment. For generations, a pastoral civilization has made its mark, hewing age-old paths in the terrain to create passageways for *la transhumance*. For more than 10,000 years, the hooves of sheep on their seasonal travels have trod these trails, climbing ever higher to the lush green pastures essential to their survival. Even today, several thousand sheep and goats spend their summers on the high-altitude plateaux in the Var and Tinée valleys.

Then there are the men and women of this mountainous region. Their "world's end" villages are enclosed universes which, once penetrated, take us on a trip back in time in a labyrinth of narrow winding streets. Their places of worship are decorated with magnificent painted frescoes, gems of Gothic art, often unsuspected behind the humble façade of modest chapels : the White Penitents' Chapels at La-Tour-sur-Tinée and Peillon, the Chapels of Saint Sébastien at Venanson, Saint Antoine at Clans, Notre-Dame-du-Bon-Cœur at Lucéram and Notre-Dame-des-Fontaines at La Brigue… Many more await your visit.

There are so many reasons to wander through the streets and little squares, around the fountains which tell the past and present of these mountain villages. More often than not, the houses are built in Alpine style, with tall façades, roofs of slate-like *lauze* or shingle, their barn-sheds or drying lofts tucked away on the very top floor.

In the Alpes-Maritimes, rural architecture is simple, even rather rough : its real originality comes from the use of tinted washes or façades decorated with trompe-l'oeil paintings, reminders of the Italian and especially Piedmontese influence. Yellow, red, blue or green, the doors and windows are frequently brightly coloured, enhanced by painted friezes and decorative patterns that compensate for the poor quality of the base materials. La Tour-sur-Tinée, Sospel, Luceram, Utelle and many other villages display beautifully decorated façades, some of which have been restored by Guy Ceppa, painter-restorer-fresco artist, and a specialist in trompe-l'oeil.

The visitor's gaze rests upon these audacious villages, real eagles' nests standing astride their rocky spurs like sentinels on guard. One soon begins to wonder why these villages were built so tightly packed together, in such difficult terrain, on land so often unproductive. They rear into view at a bend in a winding road, sometimes nestling atop the steepest promontories, sometimes clinging to the mountainside, almost melting into the mineral world around them. Most are fortified and thus bear witness to their medieval character, still fiercely preserved. The tradition of perched villages dates back to the Iron Age, though it also reflects the desire of medieval lords to gather the population around the fortress, usually built at the highest point in the neighbourhood. Other reasons include the problems involved in building at lower levels on slopes that were too abrupt, and the need to protect the community from outside aggression in whatever form it took. This type of habitat, very densely packed together, which in fact spread from the mountain region down to the coastal area, did not exclude the development of small hamlets up in the mountains, somewhat isolated and used by the mountain-folk to stay close to the pastures and their flocks. Bousieyas, for example, at an altitude of 1,445 m, is worthy of note as the highest hamlet in the Alpes-Maritimes.

The region's entire history is thus written in the soil, on the walls and at the top of those precipitous rocks... Since the Bronze Age, it has also been engraved on the smooth slabs of the mountains dominated by Mount Bego. The Vallée des Merveilles (Valley of Marvels) at the heart of the Mercantour Park is in this respect a real open-air sanctuary for the prehistoric era, offering strange rock engravings to the gaze of chamois and ibex that wander the terrain. Some 30,000 highly stylized rock engravings represent the silhouettes of animals, armed men with hands outstretched towards the sky, diverse tools doubtless portraying a civilization of farmers and sheep-rearers, in the image of their chosen land.

Sunrise with foehn effect on La Bonette at the far north-west point of the Alpes-Maritimes. From the summit, a real belvedere at an altitude of 2,860 m, one can see the entire mountain chain of L'Argentera-Mercantour.

Defensive structure on the peak of Pelousette in the "Rempart de la Tour" Massif.

Hoar-frost and a sea of clouds near the crest of the "Rempart de la Tour".

Lacs de Vens. At altitudes ranging from 2,270 m to 2,327 m, these five lakes offer hikers their azure-blue colour and inviting lawns.

Vallon de Salso Moreno, nicknamed "brown sauce" by the Spanish because of the colour of the rushing water after a storm.

High-altitude peat-bogs not far from the five lakes of Vens.

High-altitude peat-bogs near Saint-Dalmas-le-Selvage.

The hamlet of Bousieyas with its typical slate roofs ; at an altitude of 1,445 m, this is the highest village in the Alpes-Maritimes.

Lacs Morgons. In the hollow of its glacial amphitheatres, the Mercantour Park boasts almost one hundred lakes ;

deep-blue mirrors, reflecting mountain peaks and rocky crests.

On the road to Restefond the vegetation begins to change with dense larch-woods gradually giving way to vast pasturelands.

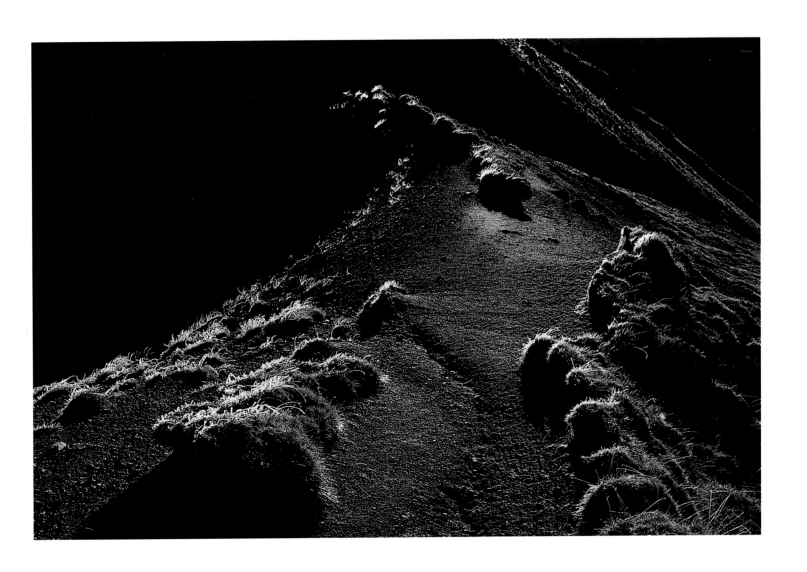

Pathway along a crest in the "Rempart de la Tour" Massif.

Chamois on its guard in the upper reaches of La Tinée.

Lacs de Laussets in the Tinée Valley.

Tinée Valley.

Cascade de Vens : yet another decor contributing to the rich diversity of the Mercantour's scenery.

33

Sheltering beneath the famous dolomite needles, the village of Péone rears up above Le Tuébi. Laid out in neat circular fashion, the tall houses of both Alpine and Italian inspiration proudly display their wrought-iron balconies, shingle roofs and loft-barns tucked away on the top floor.

Saint-Martin d'Entraunes. An ancient community in Alpine style, surrounded by a belt of shepherd's houses in an open area of natural greenery that contrasts sharply with the more arid scenery of the upper Var Valley.

Autumn landscape in the Valley of the Var.

The colour of autumn leaves matches the red shale of the famous Gorges du Daluis.

Saint-Dalmas-le-Selvage. Situated at the founthead of the River Tinée, this is a typical high-mountain village with a Romanesque church and Alpine architecture. One can just see the Romanesque church whose façade has been restored by Guy Ceppa.

Lacs de L'Estrop. Their name comes from an old Provençal term for a flock of sheep or goats at pasture ;

a reference to the pastoral activity perpetuated for generations in the Var and Tinée Valleys.

Lacs de Gialorgues, overhung by impressive wedges of stratified sandstone which support the peak of Defly and Fort Carra.

Grassy hillocks near the Gialorgues lakes.

Images of modern-day transhumance on the century-old paths of the Upper Tinée : the Alpine meadows still cling to their pastoral vocation.

Etienne the shepherd,
keeping a watchful eye
on his flocks.

Saint-Sébastien Chapel dominating the road to Pont de Clans (Tinée Valley)
in a setting of wooded mountains. Worth visiting for its 14th and 15th century murals.

On the road to Clans the mountain slopes have been carefully terraced to provide land for cultivation.

La Tour. Overlooking the River Tinée, this crest-top village owes more to Provence than to the mountains. The valley's leading commune for oil production, La Tour's prosperity derives largely from the rich fertility of its soil.

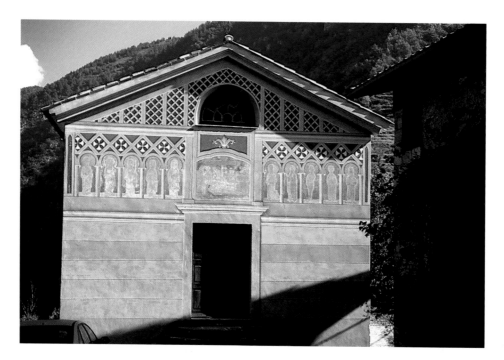

The White Penitents' Chapel with its recently restored façade in a newly created decor. Visitors can admire its frescoes, painted in the 15th century by Nadal and Brevesi, two artists from Nice.

Restored and embellished, the village of La Tour boasts very handsome houses painted in trompe-l'œil, a reminder of the Italian, and particularly Piedmontese, influence.

Bust of Sadi Carnot, painted in trompe-l'œil on the façade of the Maison Lyons (once a hospital), restored by Guy Ceppa. To make up for the poor quality of the building materials, a technique called "false painting" (pigments of mineral origin mixed with whitewash) is used to provide a decorative effect emphasizing the architectural features and giving the illusion of quality and even richness.

Ancient sheepfold on sloping ground (Tinée).

*Springtime in Marie. This small village perched on a plateau in the midst of olive-groves is a classified site.
Note the Alpine character of its tall houses, built of sombre-coloured stone.*

On the road to Le Fugeret...

Saint-Donat Chapel (Tinée).

Springtime explosion in the green pasturelands and on the wooded slopes of the commune of Val de Blore.

Typical house in the Tinée Valley, built of limestone with a slate roof of reddish-brown shale and enhanced by a terraced garden providing extra space for cultivation.

Touët-sur-Var. A village of great character, clinging to the cliff and still referred to as the "Tibetan village" or "beehive"…

A chance to cool off in the Valley of the Var.

Chamois in the Mercantour Park. Blessed with excellent eye-sight and an incomparable sense of smell, this is a magnificent animal, not easy to approach, which likes the cold and prefers north-facing locations or expanses of granular snow.

Lacs de Trécolpas (Valley of La Vésubie).

Chamois.

Ibex. Not as timid as the chamois, the ibex doesn't mind being observed and approached.

Marmot. Standing guard, with a 300° view, it soon detects any potential danger.

Clinging to the mountainside, the aptly named Belvédère surveys both La Vésubie and La Gordolasque.

Coloured wash and trompe-l'oeil painting comprise the highly typical decor of this little café in Bollène.

La Bollène-Vésubie. Harmonious unity of roofs and houses, meticulously arranged in circular fashion around the church which dominates the hillside.

Wispy cotton-tops found in summer at the edge of high-altitude lakes.

Lac Nègre. One of the region's largest lakes which owes its name to the dark blue tint of its deep-running waters.

Tende (Valley of La Roya). Its tall houses with their green-grey slate roofs and wooden balconies stand in successive tiers against the mountainside at the edge of the Roya. This is the biggest commune in the Alpes-Maritimes and a departure-point for visiting the Vallée des Merveilles.

Ancient façade at the heart of the village of Sospel which strings its old houses along both banks of the Bévéra. The town was once an obligatory passage-point on the old salt road that led from the coast all the way to Turin.

Lac Niret, on the road to the "Valley of Marvels"… almost perfect symmetry.

The Vallée des Merveilles : a grandiose site, mysterious and magical, a real open-air museum for the prehistoric era with some 30,000 rock engravings dating back to the Bronze Age, cut with primitive etching needles on smooth slabs of rock. Amongst the most famous, the "Sorcerer", arms stretched upwards, brandishing two daggers.

The altar rock with more than 1,000 engravings representing weapons, daggers, halberds, swords.

Ibex in the Mercantour Park.

*Colourful chapel
at Vievola.*

Saorge. Symbol of the village's communal life, the ancient wash-house bears witness to by-gone days.

Street dating back to the Middle Ages, in Lucéram.

Lucéram. One of the most magnificent villages in the back-country behind Nice.
Atop its rocky promontory, the tall medieval façades rear upwards, sheltering a maze of steeply sloping streets. One can also admire here the most
important collection of retables in the entire County of Nice (including one from the School of Bréa).

Peillon. A real eagle's nest perched on a peak at an altitude of 375 m and one of the finest examples of a defensive village in the Alpes-Maritimes, it has managed to preserve its medieval character.

Inside the village, the flights of steps thread their way between the houses with many vaulted passageways : a winding labyrinth that replaces streets.

Ancient tools.

*Channelling the light, the "pontis" allow the last rays of sunlight
to filter through.*

The fountain in Peillon at nightfall.

A BALCONY OVERLOOKING THE COTE D'AZUR

Framed to the north by the crests of the first chain of hills known as the Pré-Alpes, to the south by the coast and its bay, the landscape unfurls like a vast amphitheatre. From Grasse to Tourrettes-sur-Loup via Saint Jeannet or Bollène, a succession of terraces offers hikers a plunging, sweeping view of the Mediterranean coast – from as far as 20 km away.

Thanks to its protective screen of mountains, this region benefits from an extremely favourable climate. Sometimes referred to as the "immediate hinterland", it is blessed with a maximum amount of sunshine which favours particularly lush vegetation, a floral miracle of nature. Agaves and prickly pear trees, palms and cacti, not forgetting the mimosa, eucalyptus trees, violets and jasmine, are emblematic features of the area which here have found their chosen land.

« A balcony overlooking the Côte d'Azur… », – quite decidedly so because, from one spot to the next, the wanderer stumbles across breathtaking views of the shoreline with the sky reflected in the sea nearby. But here we are also in Provence : the chirping of the cicadas, the fields of lavender and olive-trees attest to that. And that's precisely the charm of this particular area, its blend of two different styles, two different aspects, intermingling their colours and savours. Slightly set back from the seaside towns, often noisy or overly garish, an authentic corner of Provence manages to merge with a Riviera which could well retrieve calm and serenity without losing anything of its basic appeal… « A Provence smelling fragrantly of musk… » as Maeterlinck so rightly described it, rooted in its sun-drenched agriculture with its vines, olive-trees and flowers, but whose pastoral tradition is giving way to craft activities, better suited to cater to the desires and feverishness of an ever-growing mass tourist industry.

A capital was needed for this particular area, a jewel in the crown to do it justice : Grasse, world capital of the perfume industry, assumed the title. It's not widely known, however, that Grasse owes its renown to a very ancient tradition, the tanning of leather. With its abundant streams, canals and wild aromatic plants, the town had originally attracted a good number of tanners who secretly perfected a technique for treating leather using crushed aromatic leaves to make the skins both waterproof and supple. And when, towards the end of the 16th century, Spain and Italy launched the fad for gloves, waistcoats and doublets of perfumed leather, the tanners of Grasse soon became specialists in the fine art of glove-making and set up the Perfumed Glove-makers' Guild… This was the start of Grasse's perfume industry. It became so successful that flower cultivation underwent rapid development in the surrounding area. Roses, jasmine, tuberoses, orange-blossom, to mention just a few, perfumed the countryside all around Grasse... Nowadays, the fields of flowers are increasingly rare, but around Plascassier, at nightfall, jasmine and roses still exude their scent, even if it is no longer, as Mauclair once described it, « almost unbearable, because of its warm and intense voluptuousness... »

In the town centre, playing host to Grasse's Provençal market, the Place aux Aires is the symbol of all the town's former economic activities. The square was refurbished at the end of the 18th century, though it is still lined with 17th and 18th century arcades whose fine residences once belonged to the master-tanners. A picturesque historic detail : at one point, the square was divided from one end to the other by a small canal carrying the town's water supply which the tanners also used to wash their skins. Little by little, the stream was covered over to get rid of the nauseating odours that pervaded the square... hardly appropriate for the « city of a thousand perfumes » !

All around Grasse you'll find the multiple facets of a landscape which arranges itself so well in pretty pictures, capturing the loveliest shades of light at each and every turn. Pictures which take us to the very heart of the back-country : to the ruins of Gréolières, Gourdon and its castle surveying the spectacular Gorges du Loup, compared by Stephen Liégeard to « a wound whose lips are eternally open », as far as Saint Jeannet sheltering beneath its impressive outcrop of granite, then on to Gattières, Le Broc and Carros, three sentinels perched high above the River Var, on again to Tourrettes-sur-Loup with its sweet-smelling violets, and finally, in the footsteps of worldwide celebrities, to the fortified walls of Saint Paul de Vence.

... Saint-Paul, for those on more intimate terms, is the archetype of a Provençal village in all its beauty, here described by one of its most devoted fans, the painter-poet Verdet :

« How delightful it is to discover the proud pyramidal silhouette of this Provençal village, crowned by its bell-tower, consolidated by its ramparts, perched on a hillside surrounded by orange-trees, with yews and cypresses that seem to stand guard over it like halberdiers ».

The village ramparts, so well preserved, date back to the 16th century, to the time when Francis 1st rewarded the villagers for having so successfully resisted the troops of Charles the Fifth of Germany. Saint-Paul was then gradually abandoned in favour of Vence and Cagnes, only to emerge from oblivion at the beginning of the 20th century when an influx of artists (Picasso, Léger, Braque, Chagall...) took a liking to the village and the exceptional quality of its light. The Colombe d'Or inn took care of the rest, thanks to Paul Roux, an inn-keeper unique in his kind, who gave free accommodation to his artist friends in exchange for one or two of their canvasses. Utrillo, Vlaminck, Renoir and Matisse were among his guests, soon followed by writers (Kipling, Maeterlinck, Morand...) and actors such as Maurice Chevalier and Mistinguette. The cinema arrived in Saint-Paul in 1941 with Prévert, soon accompanied by Carné, Kosma, Allégret and many others... The village had become, and was to stay for many years, a favourite rendez-vous for the artists and intellectuals of the day.

In the pages of this album, it is perhaps the « supreme smile of Provence », as Hallays called it, that the photographer roughly sketches out for us, rather like a painter giving a general outline, against the backcloth of the hills and villages of this little patch of land wedged between the sea and mountains.

Gattières. A hill-top village in the midst of vines and olive-trees, offering a very lovely vista of the Valley of the Var.

Le Broc. Perched on its mountain amongst terraces of olive-groves, it overlooks the Var and Estéron.

Carros and its houses huddled around a 13th-century castle.

All these small hill-top villages, still acting like guardians, provide perfect medieval settings for the region's local festivities.
Here, a fête celebrating by-gone trades and crafts at La Colle-sur-Loup.

Canadair plane flying over Saint-Jeannet, threatened by a strong Mistral wind as well as the intense heat.

Silvery cascade of olive-trees on the restanques.

95

Near Levens. Cultivated on sloping ground laid out in terraced embankments, the sacred olive-tree,
first introduced by the Greeks some 2,500 years ago, has found its land of predilection here in the Alpes-Maritimes.

Clans. Remains of an olive-grove with its highly typical barn.

Olivades in the back-country. When harvest-time arrives, coloured nets are strewn on the ground to gather the olives that are shaken off the branches.

Fire… As long as it is carefully controlled, it is an ecological way of eliminating certain parasites in cultivated areas.

Misty winter landscape (near Saint-Paul).

A caprice of Mother Nature, snow can occasionally give a totally unexpected appearance to the village of Saint-Paul.

Saint-Paul-de-Vence. Against an undulating backcloth of the hills of Vence, the most famous of the fortified medieval villages…

Vence and the harmonious layout of its elliptical confines.

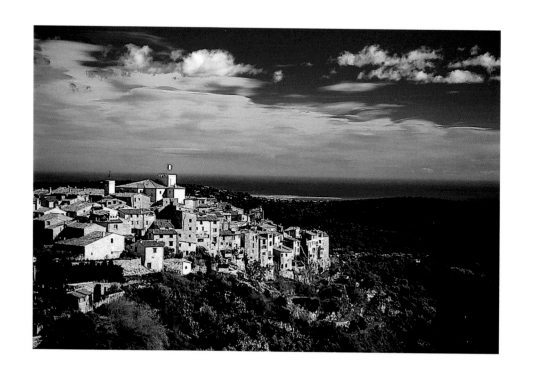

Ancient oil-mill at Tourrettes-sur-Loup.

*Tourrettes-sur-Loup,
the village of violets.
Standing on a rocky
plateau, the village
comprises a fine
medieval ensemble
whose exterior houses
serve as ramparts.*

The River Var. Down in the valleys, the rivers offer areas of welcome coolness.

Toudon.

Gréolières. Wedged at the foot of Le Cheiron, this is a Provençal-style village with pretty little squares and ogival doorways. In the background, the ruins of a major fortress recall the medieval history of the site.

Gourdon. A breath-taking eagle's nest at the tip of a rocky promontory on the Plateau of Caussols,
Gourdon surveys the Gorges du Loup from an altitude of over 500 m.

110

Sweeping view of the sea from Les Baous.

The "Saut du Loup". The River Loup has cut away deep vertical gorges and flows through vast "pot-holes" formed by glacial erosion.

In the back-country villages, time often seems to stand still.

Colourful bottles and demijohns… in the wake of Grasse's perfumes.

Grasse. Above the sweet-smelling hillsides, on the lowest slopes of the limestone plateaux, the City of Perfume unfurls its tiered gardens, while the old Provençal town huddles around narrow and often winding streets.

Façade of Grasse's International Perfumery Museum. A treasure-trove of history for members of the profession, its aim is to cover three thousand years of cosmetics, soap and perfume manufacturing all around the world.

Winding streets and colourful façades in the heart of Old Grasse. The houses, noted Stephen Liégeard,
"would end up embracing each other, if honest braces erected between them didn't make them behave in more seemly fashion"…

Jasmine stock. The most fragrant of all, the variety with large flowers of five petals, is cultivated around Grasse.

Jasmine fields near Plascassier in the countryside near Grasse. Jasmine blooms from July to October, but the flowers only open at night and have to be picked at the crack of dawn. 10,000 flowers are needed to obtain one kilo of jasmine.

*Grasse's market-place
on the Place aux Aires.*

THE COASTAL REGION

Mare nostrum... once so closely watched from the hill-tops and perched villages, for it was from the sea that danger often loomed. Today, we contemplate it, delight in it ; it is now adorned by an urban strip, thankfully relieved by parks and gardens that are often superbly endowed with luxuriant tropical vegetation.

The Côte d'Azur needs no introduction. And yet, beyond the classic images that we still retain – sand, blue sea, pines and palm-trees... plus a few parasols -, it is far from being one and the same entity. To be convinced, just take a good look around : from Menton to Théoule, wide bays with curving shorelines coexist with the wild and chiselled relief of little creeks squeezed between the Estérel's red porphyry promontories, while fishing harbours at the far end of quaysides follow hot on the heels of fashionable resorts that stretch lazily along the beaches.

Highly contrasting scenery yet again, offering many different facets, from the most traditional to the most contemporary. Baroque buildings, colourful façades – thanks to the Italian influence ! – and the wavy forms of modern-day pyramids all harmoniously blend their styles. The coastal towns compete for colour and intensity. On the façades of houses, white combines with green, which goes one better with yellow and ochre, while Italianate shutters swing slightly

open like beating wings to let the light filter through. Very often in the heart of old neighbourhoods, linen is hung out to dry on balconies and roof-terraces. Colourful markets invade little squares, displaying their citrus fruits, flowers and spices, while round the corner of a narrow street you can sample Swiss chard pie or the famous "socca" (pancakes made of chick-pea flour). Even the modern part of town has borrowed the colours of the azure Mediterranean in a search for elegance that is constantly renewed through a choice of purer forms, sometimes angular, sometimes round, in a mirror reflection of this irregular coast.

Many authors have written about the Riviera. All fervent admirers of the Côte d'Azur, they offer their impressions and images often tinted by nostalgia or amusement. Their texts serve here as perfect counterpoint to the luminous snapshots taken by Jacques Schlienger.

In *House of Mirth* (1905), Edith Wharton's heroine, Lily Bart, sees the Riviera for the very first time from an ocean liner :

« Unclouded sunlight enveloped sea and shore in a bath of purest radiancy. The purpling waters drew a sharp white line of foam at the base of the shore ; against its irregular eminences, hotels and villas flashed from the greyish verdure of olive and eucalyptus ; and the background of bare and finely-pencilled mountains quivered in a pale intensity of light.

How beautiful it was – and how she loved beauty ! »

In a short story entitled The *Lion's Skin*, Somerset Maugham sets a different tone when describing the "good old days" on the Croisette and beaches of Cannes :

« The winter passed into spring, and the gardens on the Riviera were ablaze with colour. The hillsides were primly gay with wild flowers. The spring passed into summer. In the towns along the Riviera the streets were hot with a bright, eager heat that made the blood run faster; and women walked about in great straw hats and pyjamas. The beaches were crowded. Men in trunks and women almost naked lay in the sun. In the evening the bars on the Croisette were thronged by a restless, chattering crowd as many-coloured as the flowers of spring. »

In the aptly named *Garden of Eden*, Ernest Hemingway evokes the charm of the Côte d'Azur :

« They had three rooms at the end of the long low rose-coloured Provençal house where they had stayed before. It was in the pines on the Estérel side of La Napoule. Out of the windows there was the sea and from the garden in front of the log house where they ate under the trees they could see the empty beaches, the high papyrus grass at the delta of the small river and across the bay was the white curve of Cannes with the hills and the far mountains behind. »

This evocative extract from Katherine Mansfield's *Letters and Journals* was written in Menton on September 19th, 1920 :

« As to the weather it is really heavenly weather. It is too hot for any exertion, but a breeze lifts at night, and I can't tell you what scents it brings, the smell of a full summer sea and the bay tree in the garden and the smell of lemons. After lunch today we had a sudden tremendous thunderstorm, the drops of rain were as big as marguerite daisies – the sky was all glittering with broken light – the sun a huge splash of silver. The drops were like silver fishes hanging from the trees. I drank the rain from the peach leaves and then pulled a shower bath over my head. Every violet leaf was full... »

Another extract from Katherine Mansfield's *Journal*, written on Christmas Eve, 1915 :

« The moon is rising but the reluctant day lingers upon the sea and sky. The sea is dabbled with a pink the colour of unripe cherries, and in the sky there is a flying yellow light like the wings of canaries. Very stubborn and solid are the trunks of the palm-trees. Springing from their tops the stiff green bouquets seem to cut into the evening air and among them, the blue gum trees, tall and slender with sickle-shaped leaves and drooping branches half blue, half violet. The moon is just over the mountain behind the village. The dogs know she is there; already they begin to howl and bark. The fishermen are shouting and whistling to one another as they bring in their boats, some young boys are singing in half-broken voices down by the shore, and there is a noise of children crying, little children with burnt cheeks and sand between their toes being carried home to bed... »

Finally, one of the most romantic descriptions of all is to be found in F. Scott Fitzgerald's *Tender is the Night* (1939) :

« The resplendent names – Cannes, Nice, Monte-Carlo – began to glow through their torpid camouflage, whispering of old kings come here to dine or die, of rajahs tossing Buddhas' eyes to English ballerinas, of Russian princes turning the weeks into Baltic twilights in the lost caviar days. »

The market hall
in Menton, decorated
with varnished
ceramics.

The symbol of this
chosen land, this is
what has made
Menton's reputation
as the "Capital of
Lemon Land".

Menton. Sheltered by the hillsides where citrus fruits and olive-trees are grown, the town projects onto the water the yellow and ochre tints of its Italian-style façades while the tall silhouette of its proud campanile shimmers on a tranquil sea.

Fisherman at work.

Menton. The old part of town, tucked away at the far end of the bay.

Maze of rooftops in Roquebrune.

In the purest tradition, round tiles made of red potter's clay.

Roquebrune. Detail of a façade. An azure-blue door, extending a warm welcome.

Plunging view of Roquebrune through one of the breaches in the Citadel walls.

Monaco. Clay courts,
azure blue depths.

When rooftops merge with the sea…

Panoramic view of Monaco.

Perched at an altitude of 400 m directly above the sea, the fortified village of Eze surveys the entire Riviera.

Eze. The terraced botanical gardens enrich their collections of rare plants each and every year : many different types of cacti flourish here.

137

Eze. The ghostly silhouettes of cactus plants in the botanical gardens.

Dusk on a terrace in Eze.

Villefranche-sur-Mer. Tall houses with colourful façades and green shutters rise in tiers like an amphitheatre beyond the quayside.

Bathed in sunshine, these warm façades add extra liveliness to the heart of town, creating a decor all their own.

In the mid-day heat, the flap of a shutter distils the light inside the houses.

The old part of Villefranche.

Here and there, an expanse of pebble-dash slowly crumbling away gives a glimpse of time past.

Coat-of-arms.

The Port of Villefranche, a little "corner of Paradise".

Baroque bell-tower in the Old Town of Nice.

Nice stretches out its arms to embrace the Bay of Angels.

Port Lympia, Nice.

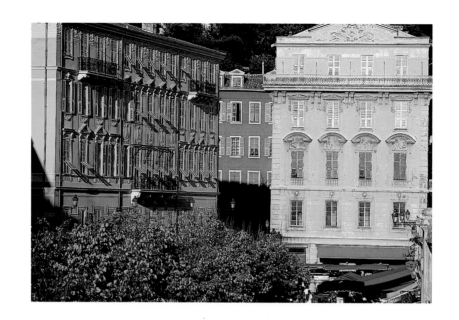

Cours Saleya, home to markets, bric à brac and cafés. The elegant promenade of the "Belle Epoque" era has today become the heart of a popular and lively neighbourhood with lots of local colour.

Port Lympia. Façades in Piedmontese style, red and ochre, embellished by Italian-style shutters.

A "patchwork" composed of the fishermen's houses of Les Ponchettes and their roof-terraces.

Striped awnings of the café terraces on Cours Saleya.

Market-day on Cours Saleya, a rendez-vous for all the savours of Provence.

Spicy colours…

Narrow streets so typical of the Old Town of Nice.

At the heart of the Old Town, an invitation to sample the specialities of Nice...

Preparing "socca". A pancake made of chick-pea flour and cooked with traditional olive-oil.

160

Blending so well with the sky above Nice, the elegant lines and bluish façades of contemporary architecture make it easy for the Arenas business centre to merge with the surrounding scenery.

The river-bed of the Paillon has become a 20th-century boulevard for Nice's theatre, Museum of Modern Art and the Acropolis Convention Centre.

Arman's monumental Music Power (superposition of double basses) graces the main entrance to Nice's modern-day version of Acropolis.

Stage-set for the Theatre.

Haut de Cagnes. The old town and Grimaldi Castle, with the snow-capped peaks of the Mercantour in the distance.

*Thanks to its port
and the fishing-boats
loaded with nets,
Le Cros-de-Cagnes has
kept its identity as a
traditional fishing
village.*

170

Cap d'Antibes.

Protected by its ramparts, the old town of Antibes slumbers on in the bluish light of early morning, whilst in the distance the mountain peaks already reflect the glow of daylight.

Mirror images in the port of Antibes.

Agave flowers on Cap d'Antibes.

Cloud of smoke announcing a forest fire in the Estérel mountains.

Lérins Islands. Pond on Saint Marguerite's Island where herons and egrets safely nest in the midst of protected nature.

Night falls over the islands.

Small creeks of white stone for a refreshing stopover on the Lérins Islands opposite Cannes.

The old part of town known as Le Suquet, overlooking the old port of Cannes.

*Bell-tower
of the Church of
Notre-Dame-de-
l'Espérance,
Le Suquet.*

Fountain at the Palais des Festivals.

The beaches of Cannes also play at being stars at Festival time.

Cannes Film Festival, 1996.

The old port.

Magnificent harmony of the Estérel's red porphyry rocks and the deep blue depths of the Mediterranean.

With its reddish hues and untamed atmosphere, the Massif de l'Estérel deploys its fragmented reliefs towards the sea in a symphony of colours where ochre blends with red and green with blue.

La Turbie. Sunset drowning in the water, setting the sea on fire like flowing lava.

Achevé d'imprimer en octobre 1996
Dépôt légal 4e trimestre 1996

Imprimé en CEE